Guitar Sonatas

By William Bay

WBM05
ISBN 978-0-9859227-9-5

© 2013 BY WILLIAM BAY
ALL RIGHTS RESERVED. INTERNATIONAL COPYRIGHT SECURED. B.M.I.

Visit us on the Web at www.williambaymusic.com

Preface

Guitar Sonatas is a collection of four extended compositions for guitar. The sonatas were composed in the keys of D, Dm, E and Em. They each reflect an array of musical moods, colors and harmonic textures. They were composed to provide concert and recital material for the flatpick or plectrum guitarist.

I began playing guitar while listening to my father, Mel Bay, performing wonderful classical pieces on his D'Angelico archtop guitar. So at an early age I heard the beautiful possibilities of the guitar played with a pick. Later I greatly enjoyed the solo works of such masters as Johnny Smith, Carl Kress, George Van Eps, Bucky Pizzarelli, Frank Vignola, Howard Alden and others. I utilized much of this musical heritage in a book I authored entitled **Masters of the Plectrum Guitar.**

I started work at Mel Bay Publications in 1968 and over the years dealt with hundreds of great guitarists and became acquainted with a diverse mixture of styles and approaches. As a culmination of the experience I gained through all those years I rewrote my father's classic **Modern Guitar Method** (now called the **Modern Guitar Method/Expanded Edition.**) In the seven volumes of that work I incorporated material designed to enable today's guitarist to grasp the technical and harmonic possibilities which would enable the plectrum guitar to be performed on the concert stage. I also authored a book which incorporated my linear compositional concepts into a text designed to facilitate reading and knowledge of the guitar fingerboard. That book is titled **Guitar Journals: Mastering the Fingerboard.** Recently I undertook to write and record a book of 25 solos called **Guitar Images** and also a recording for two plectrum guitars called **Acoustic Guitar Portraits.**

I still felt the need, however, to develop a body of musical works with the goal of creating didactic and performance material geared to making the plectrum guitar a concert instrument. It is with this task in mind that I present **Guitar Sonatas** and the other works in the **William Bay Music** catalog. .

My other books and recordings are listed at the end of this book. I hope you enjoy playing these pieces as much as I did in composing them.

William Bay

Contents

SONATA #1 In D MINOR
   1. Adagio   *4*
   2. Scherzo   *7*
   3. Allegretto   *10*

SONATA #2 In D MAJOR
   1. Allegro Con Spirito   *15*
   2. Larghetto   *20*
   3. Valse   *26*
   4. Allegro   *30*

SONATA #3 in E MINOR
   1. Waltz   *34*
   2. Invention   *38*
   3. Danza   *42*

SONATA #4 in E MAJOR
   1. Preludio   *46*
   2. Ballad   *50*
   3. Blues Breakdown   *54*

Sonata #1 in D minor
1. Adagio

Dropped D Tuning

William Bay

© 2013 by William Bay. All Rights Reserved. BMI.

2. Scherzo

Dropped D Tuning

William Bay

Sonata #2 in D Major
1. Allegro Con Spirito

Dropped D Tuning

William Bay

2. Larghetto

William Bay

Dropped D Tuning

Slowly and Freely ♩ = 58

© 2013 by William Bay. All Rights Reserved. BMI.

This page has been left blank
to avoid awkward page turns.

3. Valse

Dropped D Tuning

William Bay

4. Allegro

William Bay

© 2013 by William Bay. All Rights Reserved. BMI.

Sonata #3 in E minor
1. Waltz

William Bay

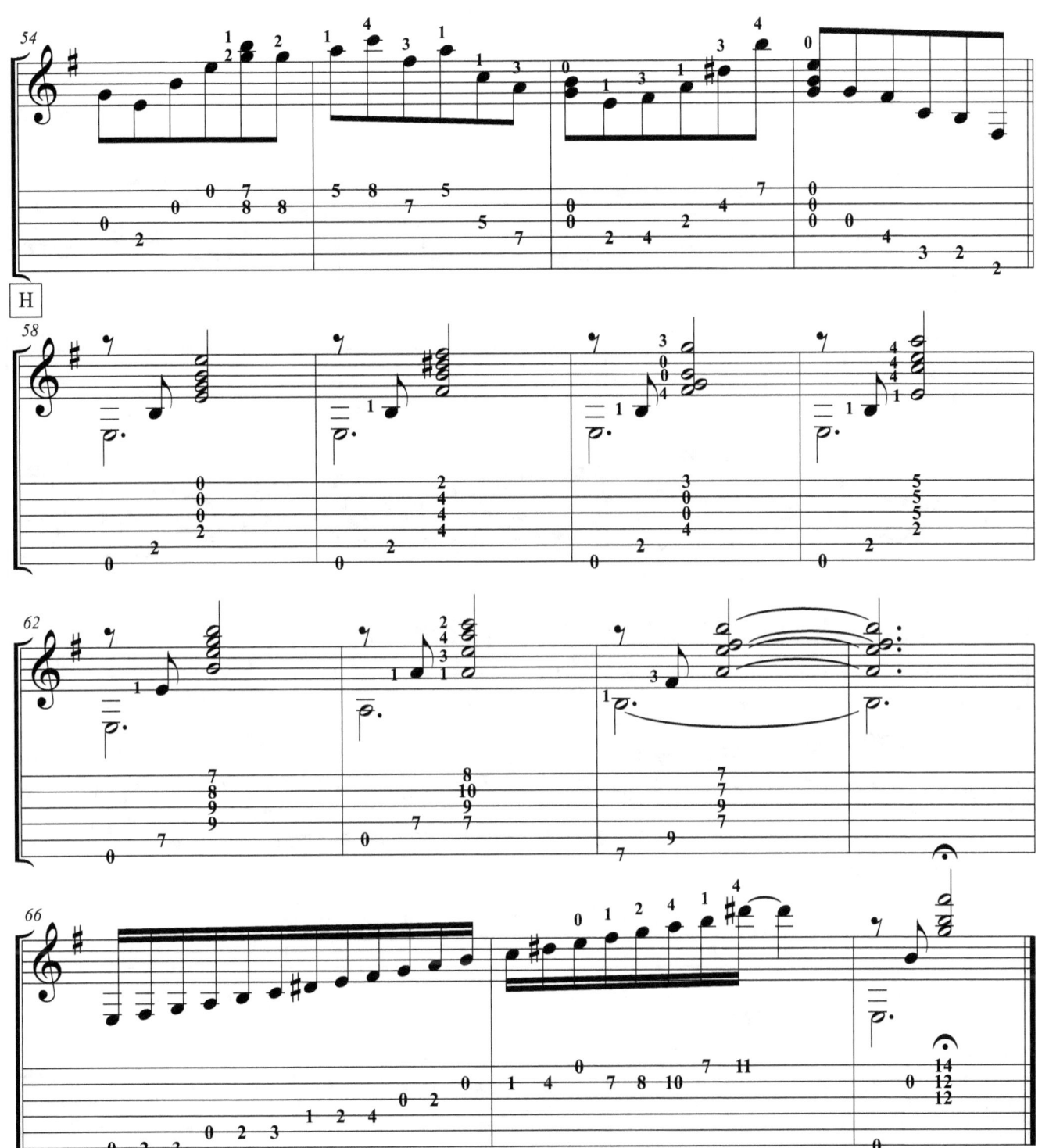

2. Invention

William Bay

© 2013 by William Bay. All Rights Reserved. BMI.

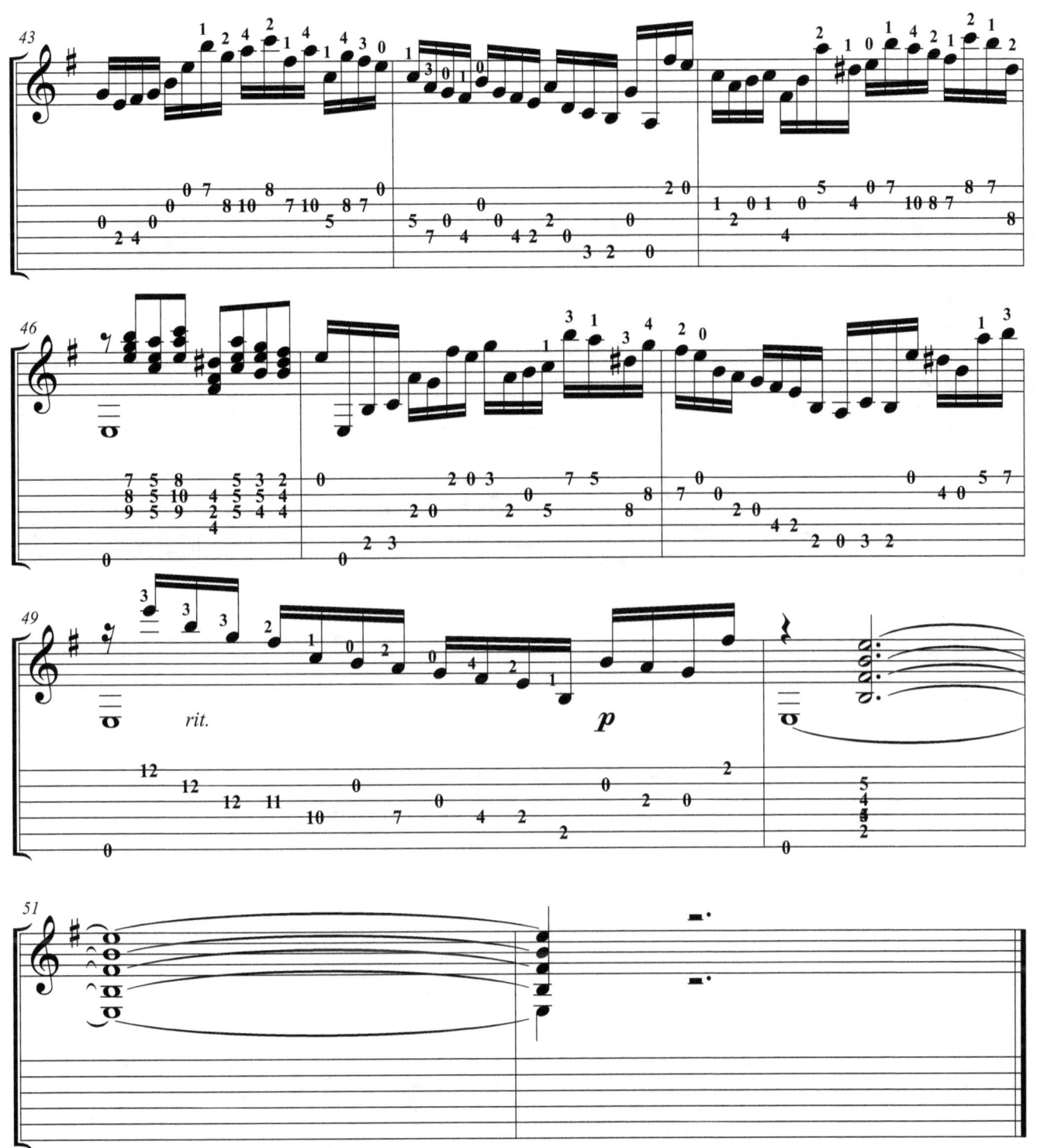

3. Danza

William Bay

Sonata #4 in E Major
1. Preludio

William Bay

Allegro ♩ = 72

2. Ballad

William Bay

3. Blues Breakdown

William Bay

Fast Blues ♩ = 100

© 2013 by William Bay. All Rights Reserved. BMI.

Books by William Bay

Plectrum Guitar

WMB02   SHORT ETUDES   978-0-9859227-2-6

WBM03   ACOUSTIC GUITAR PORTRAITS (Duets)   978-0-9859227-0-2

WBM04   CHRISTMAS GUITAR PORTRAITS (Duets)   978-0-985922719

WBM06   VELOCITY STUDIES   978-0-9859227-4-0

WBM07   PSALMS FOR GUITAR   978-0-9859227-5-7

WBM09   TECHNICAL ETUDES   978-0-9859227-6-4

WBM10   GUITAR TANGOS   978-0-9859227-7-1

Fingerstyle Guitar

WBM12   FINGERSTYLE TECHNIC   978-0-9888327-0-1

Classic Guitar

WBM08   STUDENT GUITAR ETUDES   978-0-9859227-3-3

WBM11   VELOCITY ETUDES/CLASSIC   978-0-9859227-8-8

www.williambaymusic.com

Recordings by William Bay

WBM01CD   CHRISTMAS GUITAR PORTRAITS   796279113120 (UPC)

MB11143CD   ACOUSTIC GUITAR PORTRAITS   796279112673 (UPC)

WBM02CD   PLECTRUM GUITAR ETUDES   796279113243 (UPC)

WBM07CD   PSALMS FOR GUITAR   796279113250 (UPC)

MB11142CD   GUITAR IMAGES (Double CD)   796279111423 (UPC)

www.williambaymusic.com